# New Zealand Family

Marineke Goodwin

Photographs by Chris Fairclough

A&C Black · London

Hi. My name is Joshua Taylor. I'm ten years old and I live with my family in the city of Auckland, in the North Island of New Zealand. I have two sisters: Hanna, who's eight, and Naomi, who's five. My parents' names are Vera and Greg.

Auckland is the largest city in New Zealand. It's built around the Waitemata and Manukau Harbours. There are over fifty volcanoes around Auckland, but they're extinct now, so they're unlikely to erupt. Some of the volcanoes have high cones and hollow craters, but others are hidden under rock or water.

TASMAN SEA

SOUTH ISLAND

Cook Strait

Wellington

Mt Ngauruhoe

NORTH ISLAND

0 — 100km

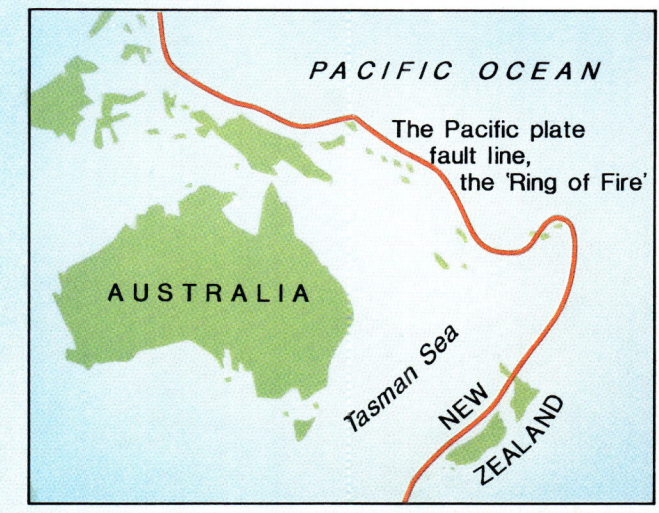

Our home is in Hillsborough, overlooking the Manukau Harbour. Sometimes, from the top of our steps, we can see cargo ships in the bay below. They sail through a deep shipping channel, on their way to and from the nearby port of Onehunga.

I think the best way to see Auckland is to climb to the top of Mount Eden, one of the highest volcanic cones in the city. My friend, Ken, calls Mount Eden by its Maori name, Maungawhau, because it was the site of an ancient Maori 'pa', or fortified village. You can still see terraces on the hillside, and the pits where food was stored.

After we've counted the mounts, or cones, of the surrounding volcanoes, we like to run down into the crater, picking up speed as we go. It's silent and eerie at the bottom. Then there's the tough climb back up to the top.

The volcanoes in New Zealand are part of the Pacific Ring of Fire. All around here, the earth's crust is thin. Molten rock in the middle of the earth is sometimes forced near to the earth's surface. In some places, the underground water is hot enough to heat homes and to cook food. At Hot Water Beach, you can dig yourself a warm bath in the sand.

Not all of our volcanoes are extinct, so scientists are always watching out for signs of volcanic activity. Ngauruhoe, a volcano in the middle of the North Island, throws up hot mud, ash and steam.

My grandfather is a builder and he helped to build our house. Our lounge faces north, so it's sunny most of the day and we have a good view of the harbour.

I have my own bedroom, and my sisters share a bedroom downstairs. Sometimes I go down there to read or to look at any new pictures they have on the walls. But if I take my friends down there, I have to warn them not to trip over all the toys on the floor.

Outside, we like to explore the bush below our garden, where the land is muddy and wild. When we've been playing by the creek at the bottom of the hill, we come home covered in mud and mosquito bites. One night, we heard a big old tree fall and crash down the hillside into the tree-ferns below. The next morning, we discovered the ideal spot for a tree house.

Dad is the manager of a pie factory. He makes sure that the factory runs smoothly and that all the pies are fresh and tasty. Dad calls in at the factory at all hours. It's never boring to go with him to watch the pies being made.

Customers telephone their orders into the office each day. That's how Dad knows how many pies to cook and whether to make them with steak, or cheese and mushrooms.

The first baker starts work at two o'clock in the morning. He prepares the pastry and beef. Then he bakes the pies in an enormous oven. The freshly baked pies are taken off the baking trays, and packed up ready to be delivered to canteens and shops all over Auckland.

The factory closes at eleven o'clock at night, when the last packers have finished loading the trucks. Throughout the night, drivers deliver pies to the customers. They get home to bed at about seven o'clock in the morning, just as I'm waking up for school.

Mum works part-time at our factory office. She used to bring home the factory laundry, which is why we always had overalls on our washing-line. Mum's very busy at home, too, preparing meals, doing the housework and shopping. She says the days aren't long enough to fit in everything she wants to do.

In the holidays, we go to the supermarket with Mum. While she chooses the groceries, we race around getting anything else she needs from the shelves. We always try to talk her into buying extra biscuits, or new yoghurt and ice-cream flavours. I think Mum prefers to shop on her own!

After school, Mum likes to hear about our day. She sticks our best stories and paintings on to the fridge door. That's also where she writes the family's time-table of comings and goings, dates for committee meetings and special events at school and church. But even after a busy day, Mum finds time to play with us – so does Dad.

Hanna, Naomi and I sometimes help in the kitchen. We like making coleslaw (cabbage salad). Naomi washes the vegetables, I chop and grate, and Hanna mixes it all together. If I don't chop fast enough, though, Hanna eats all the celery.

New Zealand is a farming country. Mum says that most of our meat, dairy produce and wool is sold overseas.

My favourite meal is roast lamb, potatoes and kumara, which is a kind of sweet potato. I'm never too full to have custard and ice-cream for dessert.

People in New Zealand tend to eat a lot of meat and dairy food. But at home, in the summer, we like to eat vegetarian meals, especially if they are made with home-grown vegetables from the garden.

We help ourselves to raw carrots, lettuce leaves, tomatoes and celery sticks. When my friend, Justin, comes to dinner, he calls it rabbit food and makes himself a honey sandwich.

When Mum runs out of time to cook, we have one of Dad's pies. He says that they're the tastiest in Auckland. But by Friday night he's seen thousands of pies, so it's a good time to ask if we can have fish and chips instead.

Mum's parents live nearby. Whenever we visit them, I always look to see if they have any new fish in their pond.

We call Mum's parents Mormar and Morfar. They came here from Denmark, just before Mum was born. They still like to speak Danish to each other, and even Dad is learning the language so that he can join in their conversations.

Dad's parents have always lived in New Zealand, but his ancestors lived in Scotland. In the nineteenth century, they travelled by ship to settle in the South Island.

People from a lot of different cultures live in New Zealand. The Maoris came here from the Polynesian Islands, over a thousand years ago. Then, much later, white settlers, such as Dad's ancestors, arrived. After the Second World War, more Europeans emigrated to New Zealand. They wanted to find jobs and to make a fresh start. Today, many people from the Pacific Islands and Asia are emigrating to New Zealand.

Morfar and Mormar still can't get used to Christmas in the sunshine. We have a tree, decorations and presents, Christmas dinner and carols. But I'm sure they would prefer to look outside and see snow.

My family is Christian, so on Christmas Day we go to church. We also meet at church on Sundays. We hear about the teachings of Jesus Christ and try to make them a part of our everyday lives. I feel close to God in quiet places like the bush, but I know He is with me wherever I am.

Our school year begins in February, the hottest month. I'm in the top class at primary school, and my teacher's name is Mr Bremner.

This term, Mr Bremner has been telling us the history of Waitangi Day, a New Zealand national holiday, held on 6th February.

In the eighteenth century, the first European settlers reached New Zealand. The Maoris called these white settlers Pakehas. The Pakehas wanted to buy the best land from the Maoris.

Then, in 1840, a special agreement called the Treaty of Waitangi was signed by some of the Maori chiefs and by Britain's representative in New Zealand, Governor William Hobson. This treaty made the land part of the British Empire.

Mr Bremner told us that the Treaty was supposed to protect Maori land and fishing rights, but that this didn't happen. Gradually, the Maoris lost their land. Some of it was sold unfairly to new settlers and some was used to pay off debts. Other land was taken without payment by the British Government. The Maoris and Pakehas fought wars over the land, and many people died.

Today, many New Zealanders feel that the Maori land rights should be recognised according to the Treaty.

At school, we are learning about 'Maoritanga', or the Maori culture and way of doing things. We study the language, especially greetings and songs. We also listen to the Maoris' legends and learn their crafts.

Mr Bremner takes us for maths and language classes in the morning, and in the afternoon we have art, music and sports classes. In the winter we play soccer, rugby or netball, but I prefer the summer sports of swimming and athletics. Our school has a pool, so that all children from the age of five can learn how to swim. Hanna's teacher, Mrs Mills, is showing the class how to move their arms in the water.

In the afternoon, children from our class take turns to be on School Patrol. We help the younger children to cross the busy road in front of our school. When I'm on duty, I decide when the road is clear enough to call, 'Signs out, cross now!' Then everyone knows that it's safe to cross.

After school, Mum sometimes sends me to the local dairy to buy a carton of milk. I often meet my friends at the Devon Dairy for an ice-cream before we go skateboarding.

Most people in New Zealand live in the North Island, where the weather is mild. In the South Island it's colder. I've never been to the South Island, but Mum and Dad will take us there when we are old enough to walk its rugged mountain and forest tracks. I'm looking forward to that trip.

In the summer holidays, we head for the sandy beaches around Auckland. I help Dad to attach the boat-trailer to the car, and when we get to the beach we all help to push the boat towards the sea.

We usually just row our dinghy around the bay and watch the yachts and windsurfers. Once we motored our little boat across to Rangitoto, an off-shore volcanic island. But the beach was so rocky that we couldn't land.

We need a bigger boat to get to the other off-shore islands. The last time we sailed out in Uncle Rick's yacht, Hanna slipped off the deck and fell into the water. She managed to stay afloat until Dad dived in to rescue her. Now Mum and Dad always make sure that we are strapped into our life-jackets before we sail away.

I always take my snorkel, mask and flippers down to the beach. It's great swimming underwater; the waves sound louder and the pebbles and shells look larger than they really are. I'd like to learn how to use scuba diving gear – then I could dive even deeper.

When a fishing-net is dragged up on to the beach, people crowd around to see what's been caught. Sometimes it's fish but often it's just seaweed. Once I helped to untangle a netful of stingrays. The biggest one was over a metre wide, and had a long barb. That afternoon, I didn't go swimming again.

At low tide, we dig for pipis. These are little white shellfish with long tongues, which live just below the sand. We feel for them under the wet sand with our fingers and toes. Later, we boil them open and eat them from their shells. They are chewy and taste a bit salty.

Hanna, Naomi and I like to go fishing. We never know whether we're going to catch bony little yellow-tails or good-sized snappers, but we eat whatever we catch.

When we 'go bush', we put on our back-packs and disappear into the wilderness. We build a bivouac, or bush tent, with poles and a plastic sheet. I have to collect old fern leaves to put under our sleeping-bags, so that the ground doesn't feel too hard.

The bush can be a noisy place. At night, the opossums make dreadful screeching noises. Opossums are furry, cat-sized creatures. They're curious enough to jump on to the tent, and they damage the trees with their claws and sharp teeth. Then, in the morning, the birds and cicadas wake us up with their loud chirping.

Mum and Dad know a lot about the wildlife of the bush. Dad says you can tell where deer have been, by the hoof prints they leave in the mud.

One very wet summer, we were stranded for a week out in the bush. The stream we needed to cross had become a raging river. Fortunately, the rain stopped before we had to hike to the emergency swing-bridge. It was a real adventure, and a holiday I'll remember for a long time.